FIRES

MICHAEL WOODS AND
MARY B. WOODS

LERNER PUBLICATIONS COMPANY
MINNEAPOLIS

To Cathleen Woods

Thanks to Alex M. Jackson, Deputy Chief of Personnel, Minneapolis Fire Department, for his help with compiling the chart information on page 35.

Editor's note: Determining the exact death toll following disasters is often difficult—if not impossible-—especially in the case of disasters that took place long ago. The authors and the editors in this series have used their best judgment in determining which figures to include.

Lerner Publications Company
A division of Lerner Publishing Group, Inc.
241 First Avenue North
Minneapolis, MN 55401 U.S.A.

Website address: www.lernerbooks.com

Library of Congress Cataloging-in-Publication Data

Woods, Michael, 1946–
    Fires / by Michael Woods and Mary B. Woods.
       p.   cm. — (Disasters up close)
    Includes bibliographical references and index.
    ISBN-13: 978-0-8225-4713-6 (lib. bdg. : alk. paper)
    ISBN-10: 0-8225-4713-9 (lib. bdg. : alk. paper)
      1. Fires—Juvenile literature. I. Woods, Mary B. (Mary Boyle), 1946– II. Title.
    III. Series: Woods, Michael, 1946– Disasters up close.
    TH9448.W67 2007
    363.37–dc22   2005017135

Manufactured in the United States of America
2 3 4 5 6 7 – DP – 13 12 11 10 09 08

Contents

Introduction

WHEN THE NEWS REPORTED A BRUSH FIRE NEAR RAMONA, CALIFORNIA, ON OCTOBER 26, 2003, NOBODY WAS TOO WORRIED. WILDFIRES HAPPENED AROUND THE STATE EVERY AUTUMN, WHEN THE LAND WAS DRY FROM SUMMER'S HEAT. EVEN THE TINIEST SPARK COULD MAKE BRITTLE GRASS BURST INTO FLAME. BUT THESE LITTLE FIRES RARELY GREW INTO SERIOUS DANGERS.

Not all fires are wildfires. Fires burned throughout New Orleans, Louisiana, after Hurricane Katrina swept through the city in 2005.

Everyone thought that this fire, too, would burn itself out before threatening people or buildings. They were wrong. Instead, the blaze joined other wildfires that were burning. Together, they formed a firestorm that roared through Southern California.

"When I woke up, everything was lit up red," said Andy Bowen, who lived in the fire's path. Huge clouds of smoke filled the sky for miles around. Schools closed. Airports delayed flights or closed completely. More than 40,000 people had to evacuate (leave for a safer area). Walls of flame up to 100 feet (30 meters) high swept over trees and houses.

More than 8,000 firefighters worked to put out the California fire. While they worked on the ground, special airplanes and helicopters dropped water onto the blazes.

The fire burned more than 300,000 acres (121,410 hectares) of land. It killed 14 people, destroyed 2,400 homes, and caused more than $1 billion in damage. It was the largest wildfire in California history. But it could have been even worse. The fire reached the outside of San Diego. If it had entered the city—home to 1.2 million people—the destruction would have been far greater.

DISASTERS = DESTRUCTION

Fires are often great disasters, events that cause massive destruction. Forest fires kill millions of trees and wild animals. They endanger the beauty of national parks and national forests.

When fires affect people, they become human disasters. Forest fires can destroy wood that could be used to build houses and to make paper and other products. People caught in forest fires may be hurt or killed. But the worst fire disasters, causing the most deaths and damage, occur in cities. A fire in a single building or ship can hurt or kill many people. And their homes, schools, and businesses may be damaged or destroyed.

A wildfire approaches a housing development.

"Within 10 minutes . . . everything I had went up in flames."

—Andy Bowen, about the 2003 Ramona, California, wildfire

What Are Fires?

FIRES ARE AMONG THE WORLD'S MOST DANGEROUS DISASTERS. A SINGLE FIRE CAN KILL OR INJURE THOUSANDS OF PEOPLE WITHIN MINUTES OR HOURS. FIRES HAVE DESTROYED HOMES, SCHOOLS, AND SKYSCRAPERS. FIRE CAN BURN CARS, SHIPS, AIRPLANES, SPACE SHUTTLES, AND ALMOST EVERYTHING ELSE THAT PEOPLE BUILD.

In the United States, fires kill and injure more people than all other disasters combined. About 5,000 people die each year in fires. More than 25,000 are injured. Fires cause almost $10 billion in damage.

One kind, wildland fires (wildfires), can wipe out everything around. These fires occur in forests and other places with wild trees, grass, or bushes. Houses and other buildings near the wild area also can burn.

PLAYING WITH FIRE

Children accidentally cause about 100,000 fires each year. They cause fires by playing with matches, lighters, and candles. These fires damage buildings and forests. They also hurt people and animals. Playing with fire is a bad idea!

Fires have caused disasters throughout history. In A.D. 64, for instance, a fire destroyed more than half of the ancient city of Rome. Fires burned down large parts of London in 1212 and again in 1666. They destroyed much of Chicago in 1871 and of San Francisco after a great earthquake in 1906.

A FORGOTTEN FOE

Years ago, people were more familiar with fire and its dangers. They made fires in their fireplaces to heat their homes. People burned wood and coal in kitchen stoves to cook. Children did homework in the light from candles and lit lamps that burned oil.

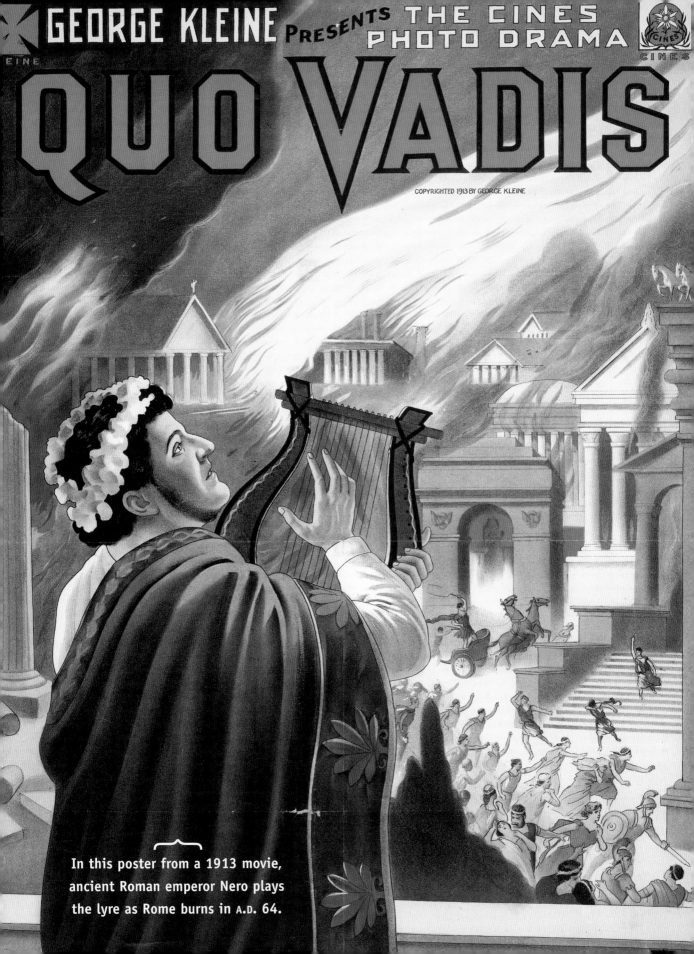

In this poster from a 1913 movie, ancient Roman emperor Nero plays the lyre as Rome burns in A.D. 64.

Most people in modern times do not make their own fires. Stoves and furnaces do so with the flick of a switch. Some people may only build a fire when they are camping or having a cookout. That change does reduce the risk of fires. But it also makes people less aware of fire's danger.

Fire is very dangerous indeed. It can cause terrible burns. And just a few minutes of breathing its smoke and gases can make a person become unconscious (pass out). Sometimes people don't realize how fast a fire can spread or how difficult fires can be to put out.

"When I was standing there and I saw those flames, I was pretty calm," said Bob Cushman. He was in a fire that killed almost 100 people in a Rhode Island nightclub in 2003. "I thought that somebody was going to get a fire extinguisher to put it out. . . . in a matter of 15 seconds, the whole stage was going up in flames."

MADE TO BE BROKEN

Fire grenades were fire extinguishers used in the 1800s and early 1900s. They were glass bottles, about the size of a grapefruit. These bottles were filled with water or liquid chemicals that put out fires. The grenades were small enough that people could throw them easily without getting near the fire. People often kept several in their homes in a rack on a wall. If a fire broke out, they grabbed one and threw it at the fire. The glass broke, releasing the liquid. These grenades did sometimes put out small fires.

ONE DISASTER LEADS TO ANOTHER

Sometimes natural disasters end up in flames. In 1906 an earthquake flattened San Francisco. The quake was scary enough. But afterward, tipped-over candles, lanterns, and stoves started a huge fire. The blaze caused more damage than the quake itself. It burned almost 30,000 buildings and destroyed much of the city. Even watery disasters such as hurricanes and floods can cause fires. In 2005 Hurricane Katrina and the flooding that followed damaged electric wires in New Orleans. Sparks from those wires set buildings on fire.

"It was so instantaneous, you have no idea...."

—an anonymous survivor of the 2003 Rhode Island nightclub fire

The charred remains of The Station nightclub in Rhode Island after a devastating fire in 2003

Other times, fires lead to other disasters. After terrorists crashed planes into New York City's World Trade Center on September 11, 2001, the jets' fuel started terrible fires. These fires melted steel beams that supported the center's twin towers, and the buildings collapsed. "It was the fire that killed the buildings," said Chris Wise, a building engineer. "Nothing on Earth could survive those temperatures with that amount of fuel burning." Fire caused most of the thousands of deaths and injuries.

Wildfires can lead to disastrous floods, mudslides, and landslides. Roots of trees and other plants help keep soil in place, especially on hillsides. When wildfires kill the plants, heavy rains don't soak into the ground. The water runs quickly off the hillsides instead. Areas below the hill may then be flooded. And rain on bare hillsides can turn soil into mud. Big sheets of mud may break loose and flow down the hill in a mudslide that destroys everything in its way. Big chunks of a bare hillside also may slide down without any rainfall, causing a landslide.

Wildfires are also a growing threat to people and buildings. More and more people are building houses near wild, untouched areas. When wildfires break out, the flames can move with amazing speed.

"You just felt a gust of hot wind," said Gary Olson, who was in the big 2003 wildfire near San Diego, California. "It was one big flame. It was moving so fast you didn't have time to think."

A VERY HELPFUL BEAR

Smokey Bear (below) was born in 1945. That was when the Forest Service (a U.S. government agency that works to protect forests) first put him on posters. In 1947 the Forest Service added the words, "Only you can prevent forest fires." People are the number one cause of forest fires. Many happen when people drop burning cigarettes in forested areas or don't put out campfires. Smokey's message has helped to prevent thousands of forest fires. Check out his website at www.smokeybear.com.

FIRE DANGER

MODERATE

TODAY!

PREVENT FOREST FIRES

The twin towers of New York City's World Trade Center went up in flames after being struck by airplanes on September 11, 2001.

London's citizens fled
the Great Fire of 1666.

1666
THE GREAT FIRE OF LONDON

In 1666 London was a bustling, crowded city of more than 500,000 people. Houses and other buildings were built very close together and were made from wood. People used dry straw to cover their floors just as people use carpets and rugs in modern times. Open flames were everywhere. They burned in oil lamps that lit houses, workshops, and schools. They crackled in fireplaces and stoves for cooking food and heating buildings.

All the ingredients for a disaster were right there.

Early on the morning of Sunday, September 2, those ingredients mixed together. And almost all of London vanished in a great fire.

The blaze started in a bakery on Pudding Lane. It spread quickly. A strong wind fanned the flames, sending showers of sparks flying onto nearby buildings. There was no fire department in those days. People had to fight fires themselves by throwing buckets of water onto the flames. This fire, however, was so hot that nobody could even get close.

Flames kept jumping from building to building. **"All the sky was of a fiery aspect, like the top of a burning oven, and the light seen above 40 miles [64 kilometers] round,"** wrote author John Evelyn. He described the sight and sound of **"10,000 houses all in one flame, the noise and cracking and thunder of the . . . flames, the shrieking of women and children."** A resident named Thomas Vincent remembered **"dazzling light and burning heat and roaring noise"** as buildings caught fire and fell down all around him.

People used ropes and axes to tear down buildings in the fire's path. They tried to make a fire break—an empty area that would keep the flames from spreading. But the fire was too big. So people grabbed what they could from their homes and escaped on foot, in wagons, and in boats on the Thames River.

The fire burned for four nights and four days. Finally, the wind died down and the fire reached less crowded parts of London. Hundreds of people used buckets of water and put the fire out at last.

The flames of the Great Fire roared through London for days.

The fire had destroyed more than 13,000 houses, 87 huge churches, and other important buildings in the city. Amazingly, less than 20 people were reported killed. But at least 100,000 were left homeless.

"London was, but is no more," said Evelyn sadly. But Londoners would rebuild their city and their lives, and London would rise again.

It made me weep to see it.

—author Samuel Pepys, describing the Great Fire of London

Not much remained of London after the fire finally died.

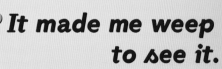

How and Why

FIRE IS THE HEAT, LIGHT, GAS, AND SMOKE GIVEN OFF AS MATERIALS BURN. BURNING IS A CHEMICAL REACTION THAT OCCURS WHEN OXYGEN IN THE AIR COMBINES VERY QUICKLY WITH OTHER MATERIALS. THIS REACTION IS ALSO CALLED COMBUSTION. MATERIALS THAT BURN ARE CALLED COMBUSTIBLE. OTHER MATERIALS, INCLUDING IRON AND ROCK, ARE FIREPROOF. THEY DO NOT BURN.

One of the most familiar signs of fire is smoke. When combustible materials such as paper and wood get hot, they release gases. Tiny bits of unburned material mix with the gases to form smoke.

"My dad and I were ready to leave for a baseball game when we saw a huge column of black and orange smoke beyond the trees," said Chris Beeler. That smoke was Beeler's first clue that a fire had started near his Oregon home in 1987.

INGREDIENTS FOR FIRE

A fire needs three ingredients to start burning. Those three things are fuel, heat, and oxygen.

The fuel can be wood, paper, or other solid materials. Liquids such as gasoline and oil also are combustible. Some gases also can fuel a fire.

To start burning, the fuel needs the second ingredient: heat. The fuel must get hot enough to catch on fire. Paper, for instance, starts burning at 451°F (233°C). Wood bursts into flame at about 500°F (260°C). A hot object, such as a burning match, can set other things on fire. Some wildfires start when lightning strikes and makes dead leaves or wood very hot.

Oxygen is fire's third ingredient. Air usually provides enough oxygen for fires to start and keep burning. But when oxygen is cut off, a fire quickly goes out.

A forest fire in southern France smolders. Though flames are very dangerous, more people die from smoke inhalation than from burns. This is because smoke from a fire contains high levels of carbon monoxide, a deadly gas.

"The trees behind my house looked like **a giant candle,** totally engulfed in flames."

—Chris Beeler, describing a 1987 Oregon wildfire

FROM FRIEND TO FLASHOVER

Fire has often been a friend to people. When humans learned to use fire thousands of years ago, they could cook food instead of eating raw meat and vegetables. Torches and lanterns allowed them to see after dark. Fire's warmth allowed them to live in new places.

In the modern world, fire provides energy for making electricity and heat. Burning fuel powers cars and airplanes. Steel and other products are made using fire.

When using fire in such ways, people keep it under control. But when fire gets out of control, it becomes one of people's worst enemies. Heat from one burning object can quickly set others on fire. Jason Hershberger experienced this danger firsthand. One night when he was ten years old, he smelled smoke in his bedroom. "It was the electric blanket that my mom put on the bed to keep me warm," Hershberger remembered. "The wires inside overheated and set the mattress on fire."

THE *HINDENBURG* DISASTER

One historic fire was a disaster for a new kind of aircraft, the airship. Airships were like the blimps that fly television cameras over modern sports stadiums. However, they were much bigger. In the 1930s, airships were the latest way to fly between the United States and Europe.

On May 6, 1937, a fire destroyed the airship *Hindenburg (above)* over New Jersey. The disaster killed 35 of the 97 people on board. "It burst into flames," said Herbert Morrison, a radio announcer who broadcast the disaster live around the country. "It's burning and it's crashing! It's crashing, terrible! . . . Oh, my! It's burning, bursting into flames and is falling." Nobody wanted to fly on airships after that. Fire made them history.

Any fire, such as this campfire, can quickly turn deadly if proper fire safety isn't practiced.

Once a fire has started, it can spread and get bigger, destroying everything in its path. Small fires can get out of control very fast. A mattress on fire, for instance, can heat up carpets, walls, and furniture. When hot, these objects give off gases that catch fire quite easily.

As the gases in a room heat up further, flashover can occur. A flashover takes place when every combustible object in the room suddenly bursts into flame. It can happen only a few minutes after a fire begins. The danger of flashover makes it very important to call 9-1-1 right away.

FIRESTORMS AND FIRE DEVILS

Firestorms happen when large outdoor fires burn out of control. Heat from these fires makes the air overhead rise in an updraft. Cold air rushes along the ground to replace the updraft. This movement of the air produces strong winds, which fan the fire with more oxygen, making it burn even hotter and spread even faster.

STOP, DROP, AND ROLL!
If your clothing ever catches on fire, don't run. Running can fan the flames and make the fire burn faster. Instead, remember the rule: STOP, DROP, and ROLL. STOP where you are. DROP to the ground (*right*). Cover your face with your hands, and ROLL over and over to smother the flames.

Firestorms occurred in the great fires that destroyed Rome, London, and Chicago. They also can occur in large forest fires. These hurricanes of fire move with a deafening roar and amazing speed.

During the Great Chicago Fire of 1871, a reporter for the *Chicago Evening Post* newspaper said the flames moved "faster than an Arab steed [horse] could gallop." John J. Healy was eight years old during that fire. He said, "I saw a great sheet of flame descend on a frame building . . . leaving a bare burned spot where the house stood just minutes before."

Big fires can also create fire devils. These burning piles of wood or

This home burned to the ground
in 1998 after a lightning strike.

other material get swept up by the strong winds. Some fire devils may be as big as cars. They soar through the air, spreading the fire even farther.

HOW FIRES HURT

Have you ever burned your fingertip by touching something hot? Imagine how much a burn all over your body would hurt. Fires can hurt people by causing burns. Burns damage the skin, as well as muscle and other tissues under the skin.

But burns are not fire's worst danger. Toxic gases released by burning materials kill more people than burns. These gases, such as carbon monoxide, can make people pass out. Then they cannot escape and may be burned to death.

Fires wreck buildings by turning wood and other combustible materials into ashes. Fires can make even brick, stone, and metal buildings crumble and collapse.

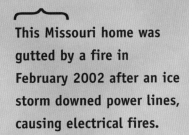

This Missouri home was gutted by a fire in February 2002 after an ice storm downed power lines, causing electrical fires.

FIRING UP GLOBAL WARMING?

Fires release the gas carbon monoxide (CO), which is dangerous to people. But fires also release carbon dioxide (CO_2), which can be dangerous to the environment. Many scientists believe that this gas causes global warming. As carbon dioxide builds up in the atmosphere, it keeps heat from escaping into space, almost like the panes of glass in a greenhouse. This "greenhouse effect" may eventually make Earth's climate too warm for life. Fires produce almost half of the carbon dioxide released into the air each year.

"**The sun shone blood-red**
through a thick haze of smoke."

—*Lloyd Head, an eyewitness to the 1906
San Francisco earthquake and fire*

A family huddled in a field during the Peshtigo Fire, hoping to escape the flames.

1871
WILDFIRE: PESHTIGO

Small forest fires were burning in many parts of Wisconsin and Michigan in late September 1871. Summer had been very dry. And fuel was everywhere. For years people who cut trees for wood and to clear the land for farming had not cleaned up after themselves. They left behind piles of dead trees and branches— perfect fuel for forest fires.

There were no special teams to fight forest fires in those days. People did it themselves. *"Father had gone out with some of the neighbors to fight fires in the forests,"* recalled Abe Leenhouts, who was five years old. *"My older brothers were busy putting out fires along fences and in brush piles. It seemed that outdoors everything was burning."*

"It was so smoky that we were all sent home and there was no

school all that week," said Edward J. Hall, who lived in the area.

Things got much worse on the night of October 8. A strong wind began blowing and fanned the fires so they burned out of control. Small fires joined together into one huge blaze. It became the worst forest fire in U.S. history.

The fires turned into a rushing mass of fire with winds blowing almost 100 miles per hour (161 km/h). As the firestorm swept toward George Foreman, he tried to escape by jumping into a well. **"The water was about 30 inches [76 centimeters] deep and cold,"** Foreman later wrote in a letter to his mother and father. **"How the fire and smoke blew down the well. I shall never forget."**

Other people jumped into rivers and ponds. They covered their heads with wet blankets and kept only their mouths above the water. But the heat was so great in some places that the water boiled.

This illustration of the Peshtigo Fire captures the chaos of trying to flee the flames.

Meanwhile, the flames destroyed towns, farms, and everything else in their path. The fire devastated an area of 2,400 square miles (6,216 sq. km). Worst of all, the fire killed more than 1,200 people. In the town of Peshtigo, Wisconsin, about 800 residents—half the population—died. For that reason, it became known as the Peshtigo Fire.

"It seemed as though the fire leaped from roof to roof, from house to house, faster than a person could run," said Charles Post. **"People had to flee for their lives, there being no time to save anything."**

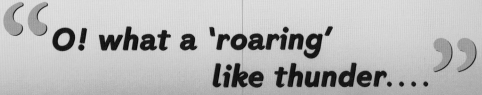

O! what a 'roaring' like thunder....

—George Foreman, recalling the sound of the Peshtigo Fire

23

Fire Country

FIRE IS DIFFERENT FROM MANY OTHER DISASTERS. FOR EXAMPLE, VOLCANOES AND EARTHQUAKES ARE A DANGER ONLY FOR PEOPLE IN SOME AREAS OF THE WORLD. OTHER DISASTERS, INCLUDING TORNADOES AND HURRICANES, OCCUR ONLY AT CERTAIN TIMES OF THE YEAR OR IN CERTAIN PLACES. AND PEOPLE OFTEN GET ADVANCE WARNING THAT THESE DISASTERS ARE ON THE WAY. FIRES, HOWEVER, CAN HAPPEN ALMOST ANYTIME, ANYWHERE—AND OFTEN THEY OFFER NO ADVANCE WARNING.

DANGER ZONES

Although fires can be unpredictable, there are certain wildfire danger zones. Wildfires often occur in states in the western and southwestern parts of the United States, including California,

A forest fire burned down much of a ponderosa pine forest in New Mexico in 1995.

GOOD FIRES?

Scientists think it may be a mistake for firefighters to put out all wildfires—especially smaller fires that do not threaten buildings. Although fires kill trees, they may be healthy for a forest in the long run. Wildfires are nature's way of clearing away dead trees and leaves, making room for new plants to grow. The young plants serve as food for animals. And fires leave behind ash that gives the soil more nutrients.

Washington, New Mexico, and Arizona. They also occur in Florida and other southeastern states.

Wildfires also usually occur during dry weather. When grass and bushes get dry, they burn easily. In California and other western states, dry weather runs from May until early November. That period is wildfire season.

But it takes more than dry weather for wildfires to occur. A spark needs to come from somewhere. Sometimes that spark is lightning. Many "dry" thunderstorms occur in the West from May to November. They have strong lightning but no rain. The lightning can set off a wildfire.

People, however, cause about nine out of ten wildfires. More people are in forests and wild areas from spring to late autumn. Their cigarette butts and campfires cause many wildfires.

A BURNING PROBLEM

In some disasters, fires burn out of control for days. But hundreds of big coal fires have been burning out of control for many years. Coal is a rocklike fuel mined from under the ground. When large amounts of coal catch on fire, the burning is very difficult and expensive to put out.

The worst ongoing coal fires are in China *(above)*, India, and Indonesia. In northern China, coal fires have burned over an area more than 400 miles (644 km) wide and 3,000 miles (4,828 km) long. The fires continue to burn up 100 million to 200 million tons (91 million to 181 million metric tons) of coal each year. They release as much air pollution each year as all the cars in the United States!

DISASTER ZONES

Fires occur all around the world. This map shows just a few of the many fire disasters that have struck over the centuries. Some were wildfires, while others burned in major cities. Fires can be caused by lightning, dry weather, or human carelessness. They can follow earthquakes or hurricanes. However they begin, fires are some of Earth's most dangerous disasters.

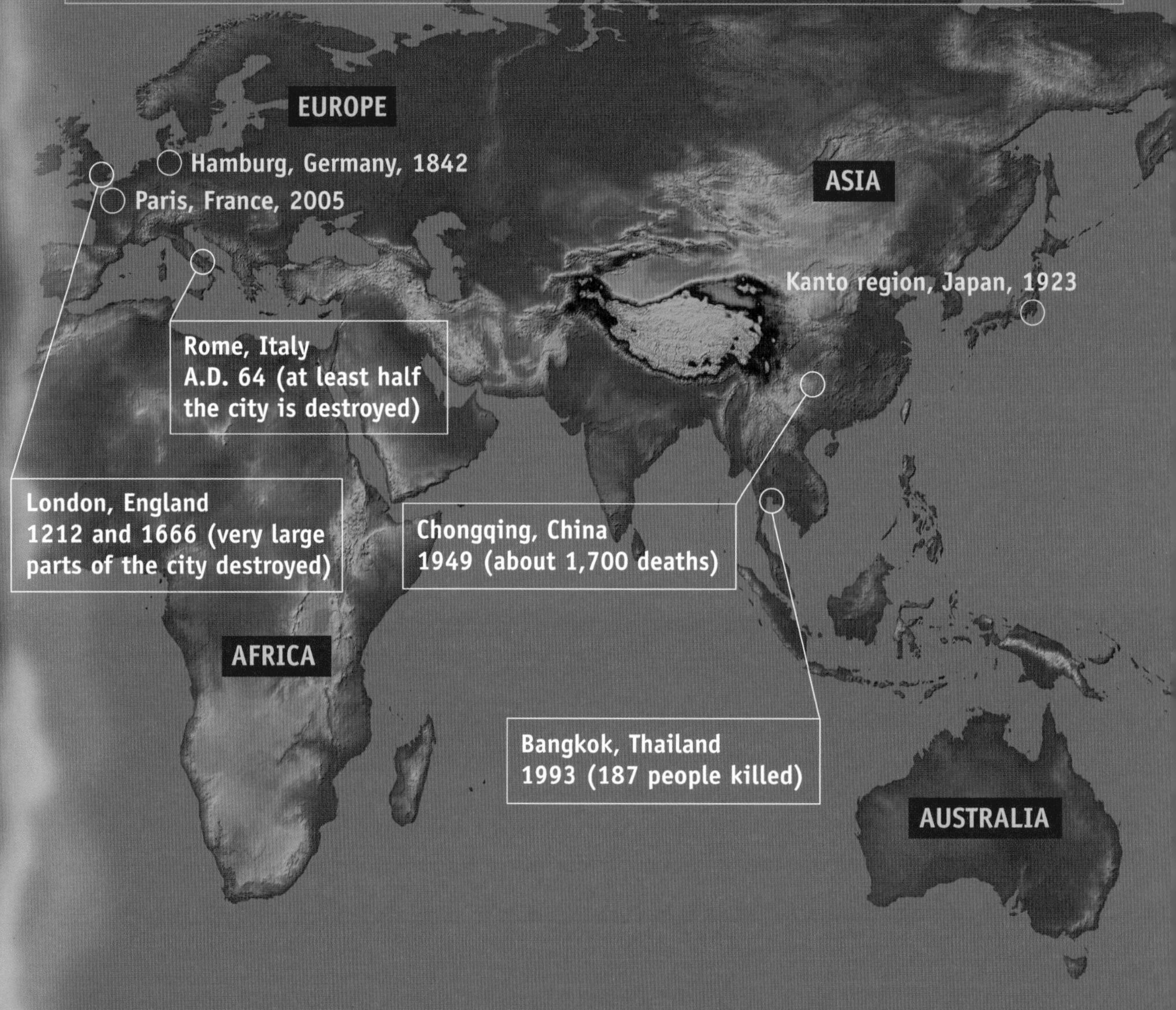

EUROPE

Hamburg, Germany, 1842

Paris, France, 2005

ASIA

Kanto region, Japan, 1923

Rome, Italy
A.D. 64 (at least half
the city is destroyed)

London, England
1212 and 1666 (very large
parts of the city destroyed)

Chongqing, China
1949 (about 1,700 deaths)

AFRICA

Bangkok, Thailand
1993 (187 people killed)

AUSTRALIA

NORTH AMERICA

Nova Scotia, Canada
1917 (At least 1,600 deaths)

Peshtigo, WI, 1871

Chicago, IL, 1871
Collinwood, OH, 1908

San Francisco, CA, 1906
Southern California, 2003

Boston, MA, 1942
West Warwick, RI, 2003

New Orleans, LA, 2005

New York, NY
2001 (more than 2,600 deaths)

East River, Manhattan, NY
1904 (more than 1,000 deaths)

Kingston, Jamaica
1980 (almost 150 people killed)

SOUTH AMERICA

Asuncion, Paraguay
2004 (more than 400 deaths)

1871
CITY FIRE: CHICAGO

This print shows what the 1871 Chicago fire looked like from the city's west side.

The dry summer of 1871—which ignited the devastating Peshtigo Fire—also caused many fires in Chicago. Chicago was a huge city even then, with almost 340,000 people living there. By the night of October 8—the very same day that the Peshtigo firestorm occurred— firefighters were exhausted. They had worked sixteen hours putting out a fire that destroyed four city blocks.

Around 9 P.M., another fire broke out in a barn owned by Catherine O'Leary. *"My husband...ran back to the bedroom,"* O'Leary remembered, *"and said 'Kate the barn is afire'."* Strong wind blew sparks onto the neighbors' houses. They caught on fire too.

The fire quickly spread toward the center of Chicago. *"Everywhere dust, smoke, flame, heat, thunder of falling walls, crackle of fire, hissing of water, shouts, roar of wind,"* a reporter for the *Chicago Evening Post* wrote. People, dogs, cats, horses, and other animals fled the flames. **"Great brown rats with beadlike eyes were ferreted out from under the sidewalks by the flames, and scurried along the streets,"** the *Post* reported.

Firefighters thought the Great Chicago Fire would never spread to buildings across the Chicago River, which runs right though the city. They thought the water would stop the flames. But the river was so polluted that grease and trash floating on top caught on fire. The flames spread even farther.

The blaze kept burning for two days. It destroyed almost one-third of the city. Before the fire, an area 4 miles (6.4 km) long and .75 miles (1.2 km) wide had more than 17,000 buildings. Afterward, there were only **"heaps of blackened bricks and dusty ashes,"** according to

> ## It was too vast, too swift, too full of smoke, too full of danger, for anybody to see it all.
>
> —Chicago Tribune editor Horace White

James W. Milner, who was there. **"You can scarcely imagine the desolation,"** he said. **"If a man wants his mind impressed with what the end of the world will be, let him come here."**

Fortunately, the fire spread slowly enough for most people to escape. About 200 to 300 people did die. But in the crowded city, the death toll could have been much higher. The damage, however, totaled more than $2 billion in modern money.

Guess whose house the Great Chicago Fire never touched? It was Mrs. O'Leary's own home! Wind spread the fire in her barn away from her house.

Many people think that a cow in the O'Leary barn started the Great Chicago Fire by kicking over a lantern. Some think that a man named Daniel Sullivan knocked over the lantern while stealing milk. However the disaster started, the Great Fire leveled large portions of the city (right).

Measuring the Disaster

WHEN A FIRE STARTS, FIREFIGHTERS MUST KNOW EXACTLY WHERE IT IS SO THAT THEY CAN GET THERE FAST. THEY ALSO WANT ANSWERS TO SEVERAL QUESTIONS. IS THE FIRE IN A HOUSE OR A SKYSCRAPER? HOW FAR HAS IT SPREAD? IS ANYONE TRAPPED INSIDE?

Firefighters battled the New York City World Trade Center fire in 2001.

That information helps fire departments send enough people and the right kind of trucks and other firefighting equipment. Two trucks with short ladders might be fine for fighting a small house fire. However, they would not be enough for a fire in a high apartment building housing hundreds of people.

FIRE ALARMS AND DETECTORS

For many years, firefighters had little information about a fire until they arrived. They learned that a fire had started when someone spotted smoke and flames in part of a city. They often had to search neighborhoods to find the exact place that was on fire.

Then, in the late 1800s, cities in the United States began putting fire alarm signal boxes along streets. These boxes were connected by wires to the nearest fire station. When people saw a fire, they pulled a handle or pressed a button in the box. When the signal arrived, firefighters could tell where the alarm box was located. They knew the fire must be nearby.

Smoke and flames towered above
Simi Valley, California, in a
wildfire in October 2003.

More firefighters and bigger trucks were sent when the alarm came from downtown. A skyscraper filled with hundreds of people might be on fire. Firefighters could also use the alarm boxes to signal for more help from the fire station if they found a bigger fire than expected.

In modern times, schools, apartments, offices, and other buildings today have their own fire alarm systems. Some houses also have these systems. They send a signal to the fire department. Firefighters instantly know where the fire is and whether it threatens a lot of people.

All homes should have smoke detectors. These safety devices make a noise when smoke is in the air. They alert people that a fire is starting. The noise is loud enough to awaken sleeping people so they can escape.

DID YOU KNOW?

Fires are the number one cause of death from poisoning. Carbon monoxide is a poisonous gas released by fires. It kills more than 2,000 people in the United States each year. Carbon monoxide is tasteless, odorless, and colorless. But it can make people unconscious and unable to escape a fire. Carbon monoxide poisoning also occurs when furnaces and other devices that burn with open flames do not work properly.

A carbon monoxide detector can help alert people to high levels of the gas in their homes. The best prevention is to have furnaces inspected. It's also important to follow directions when using devices that burn with open flames.

Smoke detectors *(left)* and carbon monoxide detectors *(right)* help save lives. Test the detectors in your home monthly!

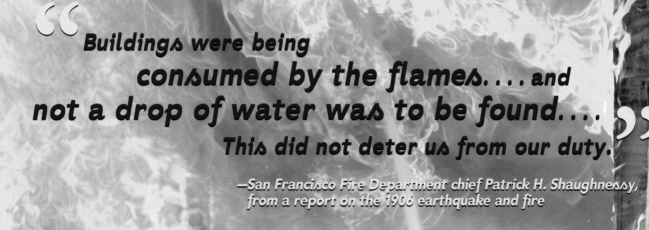

“ Buildings were being
         consumed by the flames. . . . and
not a drop of water was to be found. . . .
      This did not deter us from our duty. ”

—San Francisco Fire Department chief Patrick H. Shaughnessy,
from a report on the 1906 earthquake and fire

For more than 100 years,
U.S. firefighters have risked
their lives every day trying
to put out fires.

ALARMING FIRES

Have you ever heard the television news say that a two-alarm or four-alarm fire is burning? Fire experts use the number of alarms to measure a fire's size. When the first firefighters who arrive need help, they send the fire department a signal, called a second alarm. Then the fire becomes a two-alarm fire.

More firefighters, including those from other fire stations, rush to the scene when called by the second alarm. If the fire still spreads out of control, many more alarms may go out. They will bring more firefighters and more equipment.

FIRE WEATHER FORECASTS

Firefighters also want to know when there is a big risk of wildfires. With that information, they can prepare enough people and equipment to rush into an area if necessary.

The National Oceanic and Atmospheric Administration (NOAA) makes fire weather forecasts. This government agency includes the National Weather Service. Its fire weather forecasts alert people when weather conditions could lead to wildland fires.

Fire weather is very dry weather that makes it easy for trees and grass to burn. Other conditions, such as "dry" thunderstorms, add to the threat. Forecasters get worried when those thunderstorms occur in a wild area that is very dry.

The NOAA issues a Fire Weather Watch when conditions could result in wildfires during the next seventy-two hours. A Red Flag Warning means that conditions could result in serious fires in the next twenty-four hours. Television, radio, and newspapers carry these forecasts. They are also online at the NOAA's website.

UP IN FLAMES

In an average year, about 100,000 wildland fires occur in the United States. They burn about 4 million acres (1.6 million hectares) of land. That's an area four times the size of Rhode Island. It costs about $500 million just to fight the fires. About 16 firefighters die in the battle each year.

FIRE RESPONSE CHART

ALARMS	FIREFIGHTING RESPONSE
INITIAL CALL	FOUR RIGS: TWO FIRE ENGINES, ONE LADDER, AND ONE CHIEF CAR ELEVEN FIREFIGHTERS
1-ALARM FIRE	NINE RIGS: THREE FIRE ENGINES, ONE LADDER, ONE RESCUE RIG, TWO BATTALION CHIEFS, ONE MOBILE COMMAND, AND ONE SALVAGE RIG TWENTY-THREE FIREFIGHTERS
2-ALARM FIRE	TWELVE RIGS: FIRST ALARM PLUS TWO FIRE ENGINES, ONE LADDER, AND THE DEPUTY CHIEF THIRTY-FOUR FIREFIGHTERS
3-ALARM FIRE	SIXTEEN RIGS: SECOND ALARM PLUS THREE MORE FIRE ENGINES FORTY-THREE FIREFIGHTERS
4-ALARM FIRE	EIGHTEEN RIGS: THIRD ALARM PLUS TWO MORE FIRE ENGINES FORTY-NINE FIREFIGHTERS

Note: not all cities respond to fire alarms in the same way. The chart above is just one example of how a fire department might respond to an alarm.

This painting depicts the *General Slocum* disaster.

1904

THE GENERAL SLOCUM

The church trip started at 9 A.M. on June 15, 1904, in New York City. More than 1,300 children and their families got on board the *General Slocum*. The famous steamboat had three decks, paddlewheels, and even a live band. It took people on tours in the East River. That day, members of Saint Mark's Lutheran Church were celebrating the start of summer vacation. This group, made up mostly of German American immigrants, planned to sail to a nearby island. There they would enjoy a picnic, games, and prizes. Everyone was excited.

But the *General Slocum* never reached the island. Within an hour, more than 1,000 of its passengers would be dead from a terrible fire.

The fire may have started when a sailor dropped a match on the floor. Whatever the cause, the flames spread quickly through the wooden ship.

General Slocum sank after the fire.

Crews tried to salvage parts from the wreckage of the sunken ship.

Fourteen-year-old John Ell remembered, **"The flames spread in bursts that soon had the entire deck enveloped."** Passenger William Ortman knew it would be impossible to put out the flames. **"The boat was doomed,"** he said.

Passengers grabbed life jackets. But they were so old, rotten, and poorly made that many fell apart in people's hands. And the ship's lifeboats were fastened to the deck with strong wires that nobody could cut. People were burned alive or jumped into the cold river and drowned.

"Women were shrieking and clasping their children in their arms," said the Reverend George Haas, who was on board the *General Slocum*.

One eyewitness called the *New York World* newspaper on the telephone. **"I'm in an office overlooking the East River,"** he said. **"There's a steamboat on fire. . . . Women and children are leaping over the railing by the**

" **The fire. . . . was sweeping up from below like a tornado.** "

—William Van Schaick, captain of the General Slocum

dozens. . . . This is ghastly, horrible."

Most of the ship's passengers couldn't swim. Even those who could were hindered by their clothing. In those days, people wore their best clothing to picnics. Boys wore suits and ties, and the girls put on fine party dresses.

The *General Slocum* fire was the worst disaster on a passenger ship in U.S. history. No other fire in the United States killed more people until the World Trade Center disaster on September 11, 2001. Every year memorial services are held in New York City to honor the *Slocum* victims.

People Helping People

CAN YOU IMAGINE EMERGENCY WORKERS TRYING TO STOP AN EARTHQUAKE, TORNADO, OR FLOOD WHILE IT WAS STILL HAPPENING? IT WOULD BE IMPOSSIBLE. BUT FIREFIGHTERS AND OTHER RESCUE WORKERS DO TRY TO STOP FIRES AS THEY'RE BURNING. THAT MAKES FIRES DIFFERENT FROM OTHER DISASTERS.

Most places in the United States and other countries have fire departments to protect the lives and property of residents. Fire departments are made up of people with special training and equipment for fighting fires. These firefighters work at fire stations, which are spread throughout a city so that workers can reach a fire fast. Firefighters have special equipment for rescuing people and putting out fires.

Big cities have thousands of firefighters who work full-time. Smaller cities may have only a few dozen. Many towns depend on volunteers.

SIGNS OF THE TIMES

Insurance companies started the first fire departments in the 1700s. Each company had its own firefighters. People who bought insurance from a company attached its metal sign to their house. When a fire broke out, firefighters from several companies rushed to the scene. But they were paid only to fight fires in buildings insured by their own company. If the building had another company's sign, the firefighters just let it burn.

Firefighting has come a long way through the years. This old-fashioned fire engine was in use in the early 1900s.

Fire engines always stand ready for fire emergencies at the fire station.

These brave people get no pay and have other jobs. But when the alarm sounds, they hurry to the fire station or fire.

A RACE AGAINST TIME

Firefighters immediately rush to the scene of a fire. Sometimes they can stop a major disaster from happening. Their work may put out the fire before it spreads and causes great damage. And their work is dangerous. About 100 emergency workers die in fires each year—more than in any other disaster. In the World Trade Center disaster, 343 firefighters died.

Saving the lives of people trapped in a fire is the very first concern of firefighters. This mission is a race against time, because fires spread so fast. During the World Trade Center disaster, hundreds of firefighters ran up the stairways to rescue people trapped high in the burning skyscrapers.

A firefighter in full gear

Firefighters wear heavy coats, boots, gloves, and hats. They carry tanks of air on their backs and breathe through special face masks. The gear may weigh almost 100 pounds (45 kilograms). But it protects them against heat and gases released by the fire.

"The firemen labored like heroes," said the *Chicago Evening Post* during the Great Chicago Fire of 1871. "Grimy, dusty, hoarse, soaked with water, time after time they charged up to the blazing foe only to be driven back . . . by its increasing fierceness."

GOING HOME AGAIN

When a fire begins in a building, it is very important for people to leave as quickly and safely as possible. It's never a good idea to stop and take things from a home or other building during a fire. Getting out fast can save lives. But it also can mean losing everything.

Fires sometimes cause only a little damage to a building. People can move right back in after repairs are done. But serious fires can cause so much damage that repairs are impossible.

Forest fires raged for nearly a month in Colorado in 2002. That year was the worst fire season ever recorded in the state.

"*We hurried on, the fire madly pursuing us ...*"

—Bessie Bradwell, a witness to the Great Chicago Fire of 1871. She was thirteen years old at the time.

People may even be unable to use buildings that seem to have only a little damage. Furniture, carpets, clothing, books, beds, and walls may smell of smoke. They also may be soaking wet from the fire hoses. Mold may start growing—even inside the walls.

HELPING ONE ANOTHER

At first, fire victims need replacements for the essentials of life. They must have food, clothing, and a place to live. "You name it, we need it," said Lea Ready, who ran a donation center for victims of the 2003 forest fire in California. Her list included food, diapers, and toilet paper.

A FIRE STARTED FEMA

One fire in 1802 taught a lesson that has helped people in many other kinds of disasters. The fire destroyed much of downtown Portsmouth, New Hampshire. The U.S. Congress realized that cities needed help recovering from such disasters. Congress passed a law that started what we now know as the Federal Emergency Management Agency. FEMA works to reduce the loss of life and property in disasters and emergencies.

She also needed pet care items, such as leashes, food bowls, and beds.

Throughout history, neighbors have helped neighbors in the hours and days right after fire disasters. A. S. Chapman, who was seven years old during the Great Chicago Fire of 1871, remembered that his mom bought a lot of groceries right after this fire began. "Forty people ate breakfast with us the next morning," he said. O. W. Clapp, another Chicago resident whose house escaped damage, said, "I had invited three burnt out citizens to make our home their temporary home, which they did for several months."

People from far away also helped. Trainloads of food, clothing, and toys donated by people in New York and other cities quickly began arriving in Chicago. People in Paris, France, sent Christmas presents for Chicago's children.

Neighbors still help one another after fire disasters. However, aid organizations such as the American Red Cross have a bigger role. They help organize relief efforts so that victims get what they need as soon as possible. People who want to send money or other contributions trust relief organizations to use their gifts wisely.

A Portuguese villager offered a beverage to a firefighter after he helped extinquish a wildfire in 2005.

REBUILDING AND RECOVERING

Fire victims who have lost everything have a long road to getting their lives back. They must rebuild or repair their homes. They need new clothing and furniture. Hospitals, stores, and other businesses can face millions of dollars in damage. Cities may need tens of millions of dollars to repair the damage to buildings, roads, and other structures.

Some of the money for rebuilding and recovery comes from insurance companies. Many people buy fire insurance from these companies. If their home is damaged, the insurance company gives them money to fix it.

Government agencies also provide individuals, businesses, and cities with special loans and other help. The Federal Emergency Management Agency is the main U.S. government agency that helps in disasters. State and local agencies do the same.

People burned in fires may need weeks of treatment in the hospital. Some must have surgery many times over several years to help repair the damage. Bad burns may leave victims with scars on their faces and other parts of their bodies.

Fires also can leave emotional scars. People see and experience terrible things during fires. Family members, friends, and pets may be injured or killed. It takes time to heal after such experiences.

A TEENAGER GETS A BILL

When forest fires erupt in the United States, the Forest Service fights them. These forest firefighters don't ask questions before they put out a fire. But firefighting is very expensive. After the danger has passed, if the Forest Service can find out who started a fire, they try to make the person pay.

In 2004 the Forest Service sent a bill to an eighteen-year-old resident of Washington State. It was for $10 million! Sparks from his off-road vehicle had started a fire that destroyed thousands of acres of trees.

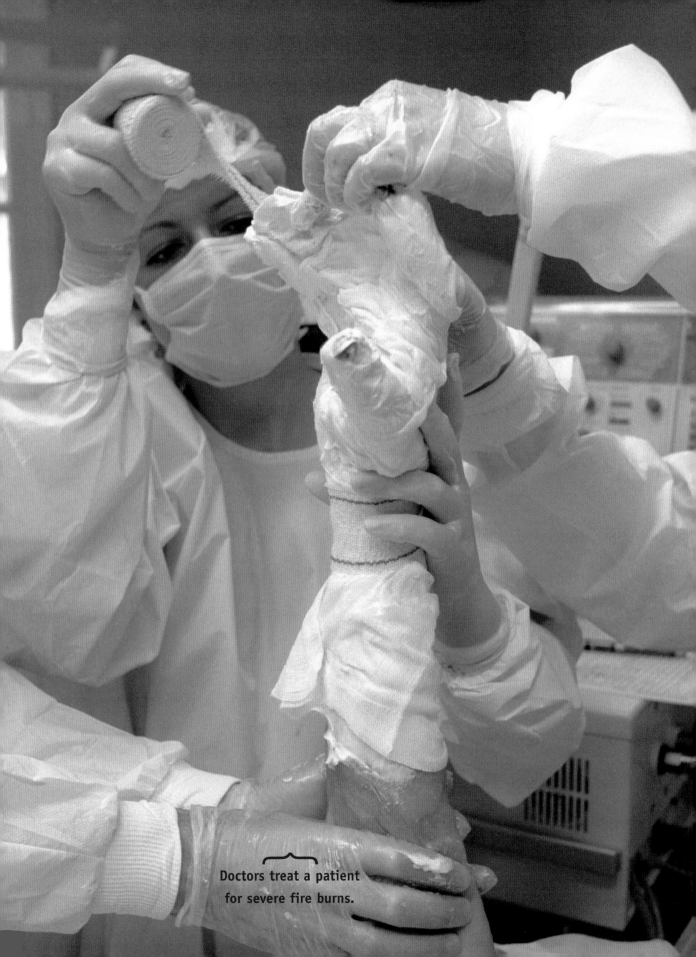

Doctors treat a patient
for severe fire burns.

2005

NIGHTS OF TRAGEDY

Firefighters suspect that the September 2005 apartment fire was started on purpose.

On the night of September 4, 2005, about 500 people were asleep in an apartment building south of Paris, France. The building was nineteen stories high. It had no modern fire alarm or sprinkler system to spray water and put out a fire. There were no fire extinguishers in the halls. The residents did not hold regular fire drills so everyone would know how to escape safely in case of a fire.

When a fire broke out in the first-floor lobby around 1 A.M., nobody knew what to do. The flames quickly filled the lobby and climbed to the other floors.

"People were screaming and wanted to jump," said Claude Camps. Camps escaped from the burning building with his wife. But 15 other people were not so lucky. They died in the fire. Many others were hurt.

"There was total panic, because we saw the bodies of people we knew," said Florence Leclerc. **"Our neighbors—a couple and their child, an entire family—are dead."**

Most of the deaths happened when people opened their apartment doors. To stay safe, always feel a door first to check for heat. But many people in the apartment did not know that heat and deadly fumes would rush in when they opened the doors.

was only one of three deadly apartment fires that happened in the Paris area in nine days. The other two hit run-down apartment buildings that housed poor people who had come to France from Africa. One of the fires killed 17 people, and the other killed 7. Only four months earlier, 24 people had died in a similar fire at a hotel where poor African immigrants lived.

Police said some of the fires might have been arson (fires started on purpose). Arson is a serious crime. It can cause disasters in which many people suffer and die.

The lobby where the fire started.

"The people who stayed inside were fine," said firefighter Alain Antonini. **"It's the people who rushed out and ran into temperatures of 300°C [572°F] . . . that gave rise to the terrible toll."**

That toll was truly terrible. But it

Many residents of the apartment buildings lost everything they had. One woman who escaped the September 4 fire was expecting a baby. She gave birth to a son in an ambulance right after getting out of the building. **"We brought nothing out with us,"** she said. **"We don't know where to go."**

47

The Future

CHECK THE DOORS IN YOUR SCHOOL. THEY SHOW THAT FIRES IN THE PAST HAVE TAUGHT LESSONS THAT CAN HELP PREVENT FUTURE DISASTERS. EXIT DOORS IN SCHOOLS OPEN *OUTWARD*, NOT INWARD. CHECK THE DOORS IN MOVIE THEATERS, STORES, AND OTHER BUILDINGS WHERE MANY PEOPLE GATHER. THEY ALL SHOULD OPEN OUTWARD.

One lesson came from a disaster in 1908. The doors in Lake View Elementary School in Collinwood, Ohio, opened inward. When a fire swept through the building on March 4, hundreds of children rushed to escape. They pushed up against the doors. There was no room to pull the doors in and open. In less than 30 minutes, 174 students and teachers died. Many bodies were piled up right at the exit doors.

This disaster led to new fire safety laws. Schools had to have doors that opened outward. They had to install fire alarms and be built from brick and other materials that do not burn. Schools also began holding fire drills so that everyone would know exactly what to do in case of a fire.

Students practice a fire drill. Drills are an important part of fire safety.

FIRE SAFETY SPREADS

Even with the new laws for schools, people still died needlessly in fire disasters in other buildings. One such disaster happened on November 28, 1942. That night about 1,000 people were enjoying music in the Cocoanut Grove nightclub in Boston, Massachusetts. When a fire broke out, some of them could not escape because of overcrowding.

Firefighters struggled to put out the Lake View Elementary School fire in 1908.

"As we ran to the exit, I looked back and saw a ball of fire."

—Liz Torres, a survivor of a 2004 fire in a supermarket in Paraguay, South America

49

Others could not see where to go because the lights went out. Almost 500 people died in the fire. About 300 bodies were piled up at the exit doors, which opened inward.

The Cocoanut Grove fire, along with other disasters, led to more fire safety laws for other public buildings. New measures included emergency lights, fire alarms, and sprinkler systems to spray water on a fire. Fire safety caught on elsewhere too. Disasters such as the *General Slocum* fire led to laws that made ships safer. Ships had to carry good life preservers and lifeboats. Passengers received information on what to do in a fire.

FIREFIGHTERS OF THE FUTURE

New inventions are also reducing the risk of disastrous fires. For instance, weather satellites are used to issue wildfire alerts. Satellites are small, unmanned spacecraft that orbit high above Earth. Instruments on these satellites can spot areas where wildfires may occur. Satellite pictures also show firefighters exactly where those fires are burning.

Special computer programs called models are also important modern tools for fighting fires. Before building a skyscraper, designers may use a model to "virtually" set it on fire. Models show how smoke and fire would spread through a building.

FIGHTING FIRE WITH FIRE

Firefighters sometimes set small fires to prevent big ones. They use these prescribed fires to get rid of dead trees and branches that could become fuel in a forest fire. Firefighters set these controlled blazes on wet days with no wind, when there is little risk of the fire spreading. Sometimes, however, these blazes do become dangerous. In 2004 a prescribed fire in Florida's Osceola National Forest raged out of control. It burned 34,000 acres (13,760 hectares) of land.

Firefighter set this controlled blaze, or backfire, to protect Thousand Oaks, California, from a wildfire in 2005.

Police, firefighters, and curious onlookers gather outside the Cocoanut Grove nightclub the night after a fire destroyed the overcrowded building in 1942.

Designers then can make changes so the fire does not spread so quickly. They may add more emergency exits or fireproof doors that stop a fire's spread. The computer program also may suggest using more sprinklers or different building materials so that people inside have more time to escape.

SAFER MATERIALS

In the future, scientists will create new materials that don't burn easily. The first widely used fireproof material was asbestos. This natural mineral crumbles into little threads. These threads can be woven into cloth to make fireproof clothing. Years ago, asbestos was also put into floor and ceiling tiles, shingles for roofs, and many other products to make them fireproof. However, asbestos is rarely used today. If it crumbles and people inhale the dust, they can get sick.

WASHING WITH FIRE

At banquets in ancient Persia (the modern country of Iran), people used napkins made of asbestos. Cleaning soiled napkins was easy. People just threw them into a fire. It burned off the grease and food without hurting the cloth.

Instead, special chemicals are used to retard (slow down) burning. Products containing these fire-retardant materials will burn. But they burn more slowly and release less heat and poisonous gas. That gives people more time to escape a fire. Fire-retardant materials are used in carpets, the plastic in television sets and computers, furniture, wood for building houses, and many other products that fuel fires.

Fire-retardant material in a mattress may have saved ten-year-old Jason Hershberger's house. When an electric blanket set his mattress on fire, the mattress smoldered (burned slowly). "If it had burst into flames," Hershberger said, "the whole house could have caught on fire."

STURDIER SKELETONS

Scientists also work to create better materials to insulate (protect from heat) the steel beams inside skyscrapers and other buildings. The beams are a building's skeleton. They hold up the whole building. If a fire is hot enough to melt the beams, the building will collapse.

A firefighting helicopter dropped water on a burning house. The house was destroyed by the 2003 wildfire in San Diego County, California.

Builders spray steel beams with concrete or foamlike material that keeps the heat out for a while. But they need new, better materials. Better insulation would not have saved the World Trade Center. But it might have kept the towers standing longer, allowing more people to escape.

Scientists also are looking for better materials to put out fires. Water puts out fires by cooling the burning material and cutting off oxygen. But water may spread fires involving grease, gasoline, and certain other materials. These materials float on the water and continue burning. As the water flows away, it can spread the flames. For these fires, firefighters use powdered materials and gases that cut off the oxygen supply.

FIRE PREVENTION AT HOME

There are many ways of preventing a fire disaster in your own home. About half of all serious home fires occur when everyone is asleep. That makes it especially important to have smoke detectors.

Many home fires start in the kitchen. Sparks from fireplaces, woodstoves, and power tools also start fires. It is important to keep a small fire extinguisher near these things. Make sure that family members know how to use the extinguisher. And make sure they call the fire department. People should never try to put out a major fire by themselves.

Fire can be dangerous and frightening. Throughout history, they have caused many great disasters. But knowing more about fires can help protect you and your family from future fire disasters.

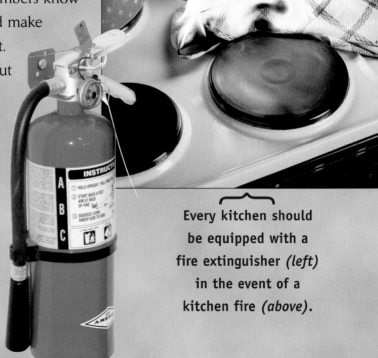

Every kitchen should be equipped with a fire extinguisher (left) in the event of a kitchen fire (above).

You and your family should have a plan in case of a fire emergency in your home. Here are some basic rules

Know two ways out of every room in your house. If one is blocked, use the other.

If there is smoke in the room, crawl under it.

Feel each door in the house before opening it. If the door is hot, use another escape route.

If the door is cool, open it slowly. If smoke and hot air pour in, slam the door shut and use another escape route.

Agree on a spot outside where everyone will meet. Then you will know whether anyone is left inside.

Timeline

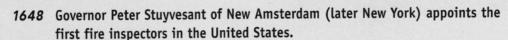

356 B.C. A fire destroys the Temple of Artemis at Ephesus in Turkey.

A.D. 64 The ruler Nero watches as a huge fire destroys more than half of Rome *(right)*.

1212 Fire burns much of London.

1648 Governor Peter Stuyvesant of New Amsterdam (later New York) appoints the first fire inspectors in the United States.

1666 The Great Fire of London destroys Saint Paul's Cathedral and most of the rest of the city.

1800 The British warship *Queen Charlotte* catches fire, killing 700 crew members.

1802 Much of downtown Portsmouth, New Hampshire, is destroyed in a fire. The disaster prompts the U.S. Congress to pass a law founding what we now know as the Federal Emergency Management Agency (FEMA).

1842 Fire burns for 100 hours in Hamburg, Germany, destroying half of the city.

1865 The steamship *Sultana* explodes, killing between 1,400 and 1,700 former Union (Northern) prisoners of the U.S. Civil War (1861–1865).

1871 More than 17,000 buildings are destroyed in the Great Chicago Fire. On the same day as the Chicago fire, a forest fire near Peshtigo, Wisconsin, kills half the town's citizens—more than 800 people.

1904 Less than one month after the Iroquois Theater opens in Chicago, a fire there kills more than 600 people.

1904 The steamboat *General Slocum* catches fire. More than 1,000 people are killed.

1906 A major earthquake in San Francisco knocks over cooking stoves, igniting a devastating fire that kills thousands *(left)*.

1908 A fire at Lake View Elementary School in Collinwood, Ohio, kills 172 students, 2 teachers, and a rescuer when they are trapped at the exit doors.

1911 The Triangle Shirtwaist Factory fire in New York City kills almost 150 young women workers. The disaster leads to reforms in fire and building codes.

1917 A military supply ship explodes in Nova Scotia, Canada, killing at least 1,600 people.

1923 An earthquake in Japan results in 88 separate fires and firestorms, killing 100,000 people.

1934 The cruise ship *Morro Castle* catches fire off the New Jersey coast, killing 137 people. Crew members took most of the spots in the lifeboats.

1937 The airship *Hindenburg* catches fire and explodes in only 40 seconds.

1942 Boston's Cocoanut Grove nightclub is destroyed by fire. Almost 500 people die.

1944 A circus tent catches fire during a performance of the Ringling Brothers and Barnum and Bailey Circus in Hartford, Connecticut *(right)*, killing 168 people.

1945 Smokey Bear is born as a symbol to help prevent forest fires.

1949 About 1,700 people are killed when the waterfront of Chongqing, China, is damaged in a fire. A fire ignites inside the *Apollo* 1 spacecraft, killing the 3 astronauts performing tests on the craft.

1980 Nearly 150 residents of a Kingston, Jamaica, home for the elderly die in a fire.

1987 Severe forest fires in northern China and southern Siberia, Russia, burn more than 2,813 square miles (7,286 sq. km) of land and kill close to 200 people.

1993 The world's deadliest factory fire breaks out in a doll factory in Bangkok, Thailand *(left)*, killing 187 people.

2001 Terrorists crash a jetliner into the World Trade Center in New York City. Jet fuel begins a fire that melts the twin towers' steel beams, causing them to collapse, and killing more than 2,600 people.

2003 In Rhode Island, the Station nightclub goes up in flames after concert special effects using fire go wrong. About 100 people die. Huge wildfires roar through Southern California.

2004 A fire in a supermarket in Paraguay, South America, kills more than 400 people.

2005 Hurricane Katrina damages electric wires in New Orleans. Sparks from the wires set buildings on fire.

2006 During Nepal's dry season, a series of fires breaks out, killing about 10 people and leaving hundreds homeless.

Glossary

asbestos: a highly fire resistant mineral that was once widely used in fireproofing, especially in buildings. However, scientists have discovered that asbestos is carcinogenic (cancer-causing), and it is no longer used.

carbon monoxide: a colorless, odorless gas that is released as material burns. Carbon monoxide is poisonous and can cause people to become unconscious.

combustion: the chemical reaction of burning. Materials that burn are called combustible.

computer model: a computer program that shows, or models, the way an event might unfold. For example, a computer model showing how a major fire would affect a building can help planners make the structure safer.

dry thunderstorm: a storm that produces lightning but no rain. Dry thunderstorms can cause wildfires if lightning strikes dry grass or other materials.

fire break: a barrier or empty space created to keep a fire from spreading

fire devil: a burning pile of wood or other material that gets swept up by the strong winds. Fire devils then soar through the air, spreading the fire even farther.

fire extinguisher: a piece of equipment that sprays out chemicals to put out a fire

fireproof: mostly or fully resistant to burning

fire-retardant: resistant to fire. Fire-retardant materials do burn, but much more slowly than other materials. Fire-retardant goods are also sometimes called flame-retardant.

firestorm: a raging, quickly moving mass of fire that can form when an outdoor fire burns out of control

flashover: a type of fire that occurs when temperatures reach such a high level that every combustible object in a room suddenly bursts into flame

prescribed burning: the careful and controlled burning of wild land in order to prevent a larger and more destructive fire

smoke detector: a safety device that makes a noise when smoke is in the air, to alert people that a fire is burning

weather satellite: an unmanned spacecraft that orbits Earth, taking pictures and monitoring weather. Instruments on these satellites can spot areas where wildfires may begin, as well as show where fires are already burning.

wildfire: a fire that burns in a forest or on other wild land

Places to Visit

Chicago Historical Society

http://www.chicagohs.org/
Visit this site to learn about the history of Chicago and to see exhibits on the devastating fire of 1871.

Cincinnati Fire Museum

http://www.cincyfiremuseum.com/
Located in Cincinnati, Ohio, this museum receives more than 25,000 visitors each year. You can see leather fire buckets, a gigantic fire drum, and an 1836 hand pumper.

Hall of Flame Museum of Firefighting

http://www.hallofflame.org/
Located in Phoenix, Arizona, this museum has fire apparatus on display, dating from 1725 to 1969. It is sponsored by the National Historical Fire Foundation.

New York City Fire Museum

http://www.nycfiremuseum.org/index.php
You'll find a large collection of firefighting equipment here, going back to colonial times.

Peshtigo Fire Museum

http://www.peshtigotimes.com/FireMuseum.html
Located in Peshtigo, Wisconsin, this museum contains articles about the town history, survivor stories, and a huge painting showing the survivors seeking safety in the river.

San Francisco Fire Museum

http://www.sffiremuseum.org/
There were at least five large fires in San Francisco, California, before the 1906 earthquake and fire. Many souvenirs of volunteer and professional firefighters can be found here.

Source Notes

4 Lynn Vincent, "The San Diego Wildfires: A Local Church Redeems Disaster Relief," *Capital Research Center*, January 2004, http://www.capitalresearch.org/pubs/pdf/01_04_CC.pdf (December 20, 2005).

5 Ibid.

8 Cable News Network, "Nightclub Fire Survivor Calls on Congress to Act," *CNN.com*, March 13, 2003, http://edition.cnn.com/2003/ALLPOLITICS/03/13/nightclub.fire.ap (December 20, 2005).

9 Michael Hammerschlag, "Hells Kitchen: Nightclub Fire at the Station," *Hammernews.com*, February 2003, http://hammernews.com/nightclub.htm (March 14, 2006).

10 Sheila Barter, "How the World Trade Center Fell," *BBC News: Americas*, September 13, 2001, http://public-action.com/911/jmcm/BBCNews/ (December 20, 2005).

10 Cable News Network, "Fire Fatalities Underestimated Flame Speed," *CNN.com*, October 28, 2003, http://edition.cnn.com/2003/US/West/10/28/wildfire.deaths.ap (December 20, 2005).

12–13 "Fire," *channel4.com*, n.d., http://www.channel4.com/history/microsites/H/history/fire/story1.html (December 21, 2005).

13 Ibid.

13 Ibid.

13 "The Great Fire of London, 1666," *EyeWitness to History*, 2004, http://www.eyewitnesstohistory.com (December 21, 2005).

14 Christopher Beeler, personal interview with the authors, November 12, 2004, Benjamin Franklin International School, Barcelona, Spain.

15 Ibid.

16 Wikipedia contributors, "Herbert Morrison (announcer)," *Wikipedia: The Free Encyclopedia*, December 12, 2005, http://en.wikipedia.org/wiki/Herbert_Morrison_%28announcer%29 (December 21, 2005).

16 Jason Hershberger, personal interview with the authors, November 14, 2004, Barcelona, Spain.

18 Chicago Historical Society and the Trustees of Northwestern University, "Media Event: The Adamantine Bulwarks of Hell," *The Great Chicago Fire and the Web of Memory*, 1996, http://www.chicagohistory.org/fire/media/bulwark.html (December 21, 2005).

18 Chicago Historical Society and the Trustees of Northwestern University, "An Anthology of Fire Narratives: John J. Healy," *The Great Chicago Fire and the Web of Memory*, 1996, http://www.chicagohs.org/fire/witnesses/healy.html (December 21, 2005).

21 Lloyd Head, "One Boy's Experience: A Member of the Roosevelt Boys' Club Writes of His Experience during and after the Great Earthquake," *Virtual Museum of the City of San Francisco–The Great 1906 Earthquake and Fire*, n.d., http://www.sfmuseum.net/1906/ew7.html (February 1, 2006).

22 MSU College of Social Science and Department of Geography, *Major Post-Logging Fires in Michigan: The 1800s*, n.d., http://web.archive.org/web/20031230090541/http://www.geo.msu.edu/geo333/fires.html (December 30, 2005).

22 Oconto County WIGenWeb Project, "Fearful Days," *Peshtigo Fire Page*, n.d., http://www.rootsweb.com/~wioconto/firehall.htm (December 21, 2005).

23 Oconto County WIGenWeb Project, "Fire Letter," *Peshtigo Fire Page*, n.d., http://www.rootsweb.com/~wioconto/fireletter.htm (December 21, 2005).

23 MSU College of Social Science and Department of Geography, *Major Post-Logging Fires.*

23 "Fire Letter."

28 Chicago Historical Society and the Trustees of Northwestern University, "The O'Leary Legend: Kate the Barn is Afire," *The Great Chicago Fire and the Web of Memory*, 1996, http://www.chicagohs.org/fire/oleary/kate.html (December 21, 2005).

28–29 Chicago Historical Society and the Trustees of Northwestern University, "Media Event: The Adamantine Bulwarks of Hell."

29 Chicago Historical Society and the Trustees of Northwestern University, "An Anthology of Fire Narratives: James W. Milner," *The Great Chicago Fire and the Web of Memory*, 1996, http://www.chicagohs.org/fire/witnesses/milner.html (December 21, 2005).

29 Chicago Historical Society and the Trustees of Northwestern University, "The Eyewitnesses," *The Great Chicago Fire and the Web of Memory*, 1996, http://www.chicagohs.org/fire/witnesses/essay-2.html (December 21, 2005).

33 Patrick H. Shaughnessy, "Report on the 1906 Earthquake and Fire," *Virtual Museum of the City of San Francisco–The Great 1906 Earthquake and Fire*, n.d., http://www.sfmuseum.net/conflag/cod.html (February 1, 2006).

36 Edward O' Donnell, *Ship Ablaze: The Tragedy of the Steamboat General Slocum* (New York: Broadway Books, 2003), 130.

36 Ibid., 105.

37 Ibid., 117.

37 Ibid., 146.

37 O' Donnell, 107.

40 Chicago Historical Society and the Trustees of Northwestern University, "Media Event: The Adamantine Bulwarks of Hell."

41 Chicago Historical Society and the Trustees of Northwestern University, "An Anthology of Fire Narratives: Bessie Bradwell," *The Great Chicago Fire and the Web of Memory*, 1996, http://www.chicagohs.org/fire/witnesses/bradwell.html (December 21, 2005).

42 SignOnSanDiego staff, "Firestorm 2003: News in Brief," *SignOnSanDiego.com*, February 3, 2004, http://www.signonsandiego.com/news/weblogs/fires/index.html (December 21, 2005).

42 Chicago Historical Society and the Trustees of Northwestern University, "An Anthology of Fire Narratives: A. S. Chapman," *The Great Chicago Fire and the Web of Memory*, 1996, http://www.chicagohs.org/fire/witnesses/chapman.html (December 21, 2005).

42 Chicago Historical Society and the Trustees of Northwestern University, "An Anthology of Fire Narratives: O. W. Clapp," *The Great Chicago Fire and the Web of Memory*, 1996, http://www.chicagohs.org/fire/witnesses/clapp.html (December 21, 2005).

46 Cecile Brisson, "Fire in Housing Project South of Paris Kills 15," *SignOnSanDiego.com*, September 4, 2005, http://signonsandiego.com/news/world/20050904-1355-france-fire.html (December 21, 2005).

46 AFP, "Arson Blamed as New Paris Fire Kills 15," *Sydney Morning Herald Online*, September 5, 2005, http://smh.com.au/news/world/arson-blamed-as-new-paris-fire-kills-15/2005/09/05/1125772438326.html?oneclick=true (December 21, 2005).

47 "14 Killed in Third Big Paris Fire, Arson Suspected," *SABC News*, September 4, 2005, http://www.sabcnews.co.za/world/europe/0,2172,111714,00.html (December 21, 2005).

47 Cecile Brisson, "Fire in Housing Project."

49 Reuters, "Paraguay Fire Tragedy Toll Rises to 300," *DAWN.com*, August 2, 2004, http://www.dawn.com/2004/08/03/int11.htm (February 1, 2006).

52 Jason Hershberger, personal interview.

Selected Bibliography

Duey, Kathleen. *More Freaky Facts about Natural Disasters*. New York: Aladdin Paperbacks, 2000.

Fuller, Margaret. *Forest Fires: An Introduction to Wildland Fire Behavior, Management, Firefighting, and Prevention*. New York: Wiley, 1991.

Gess, Denise. *Firestorm at Peshtigo: A Town, Its People, and the Deadliest Fire in American History*. New York: Henry Holt, 2002.

Goodman, Edward C. *Fire!: The 100 Most Devastating Fires and the Heroes Who Fought Them*. New York: Black Dog & Leventhal, 2001.

Leschak, Peter M. *Ghosts of the Fireground: Echoes of the Great Peshtigo Fire and the Calling of a Wildland Firefighter*. San Francisco: HarperSanFrancisco, 2002.

Maloney, William Edward. *The Great Disasters*. New York: Grosset & Dunlap, 1976.

Markels, Alex. "Cutting Through Smoke." *U.S.News & World Report*, August 30, 2004, 28.

Newton, David E. *Encyclopedia of Fire*. Westport, CT: Oryx Press, 2002.

Pyne, Stephen J. *Fire: A Brief History*. Seattle: University of Washington Press, 2001.

Spotts, Peter N. "After the Flames." *Christian Science Monitor*, November 6, 2003, 14.

Further Resources

BOOKS

Alagna, Magdalena. *The Great Fire of London of 1666*. New York: Rosen Publishing Group, 2004. Learn more about the fire that destroyed London in 1666.

Crew, Linda. *Fire on the Wind*. New York: Delacorte Press, 1995. In this historical novel for older readers, thirteen-year-old Estora witnesses the 1933 Tillamook forest fire in Oregon.

Duey, K., and K. A. Bale. *Forest Fire, Hinckley, Minnesota, 1894*. New York: Aladdin Paperbacks, 1999. In this novel, Carrie and Daniel must find a way to escape a fire raging in northern Minnesota.

Fall, Mitchell. *Careers in Fire Departments' Search and Rescue Units*. New York: Rosen Publishing Group, 2003. Find out how you can be a firefighter.

Haas, Jessie. *Fire! My Parents Story*. New York: Greenwillow Books, 1998. This is a true story of a fire that sweeps through a Vermont house and led to the start of a volunteer fire department in this rural area.

Holden, Henry M. *Fire-Fighting Aircraft and Smoke Jumpers*. Berkeley Heights, NJ: Enslow Publishers, 2002. Take an up close look at some of the specialized equipment used to fight fires.

Littlefield, Holly. *Fire at the Triangle Factory*. Minneapolis: Millbrook Press, 1996. This historical novel examines the 1911 Triangle Shirtwaist Factory fire.

Murphy, Jim. *The Great Fire*. New York: Scholastic, Inc., 1995. This award-winning book uses primary sources to take a new look at the Great Chicago Fire.

Patent, Dorothy Hinshaw. *Fire, Friend or Foe*. New York: Clarion Books, 1998. This book provides an overview of how fires start and burn, how they can help and hurt the environment, and how well or poorly fire management programs work.

Ransom, Candace. *Fire in the Sky*. Minneapolis: Carolrhoda Books, 1997. This novel explores the Hidenburg airship disaster through the eyes of a young boy.

Southall, Ivan. *Ash Road*. Asheville, NC: Front Street, 2004. This novel tells the story of three boys who accidentally start a wildfire in the dry Australian countryside.

Woods, Michael, and Mary B. Woods. *Earthquakes*. Minneapolis: Lerner Publications Company, 2007. Learn more about earthquakes, a common cause of fires.

Woods, Michael, and Mary B. Woods. *Volcanoes*. Minneapolis: Lerner Publications Company, 2007. Read all about volcanic eruptions, including what causes them, where they occur, and how they affect people's lives.

WEBSITES & MOVIES

Fire Call: A Wildland Firefighter Speaks
http://www.nationalgeographic.com/firecall
At this site from National Geographic, read the story of a real wildland firefighter.

Fire Weather Forecasts
http://www.spc.noaa.gov/products/fire_wx/
At this site, the National Weather Service's Storm Prediction Center provides up-to-date information about fire forecast areas.

Kern County Fire Department–Interactive Media
http://www.co.kern.ca.us/fire/media/index.htm
Visit this site to take a virtual tour, see inside a new fire truck, and learn about firefighting equipment.

Smokey Bear
http://www.smokeybear.com/
Smokey's modern slogan is "Only you can prevent wildfires." Visit the kids' section of Smokey's page for games, fast facts, and more.

U.S. Fire Administration for Kids
http://usfa.fema.gov/kids
The Kids Page at the U.S. Fire Administration offers tips on how you can help your family prevent fires.

Be sure to take the test to become a junior fire marshal. Also visit http://www.fema.gov/kids/wldfire.htm to take a wildfire math challenge and find information on keeping pets safe from fires.

Firefight: Stories from the Frontlines. VHS. Directed by David Wittkower. Studio City, CA: 44 Blue Productions, 1999. See the disastrous effects of wildfires and watch as firefighters battle the flames.

Nova: Fire Wars. DVD. Directed by Kirk Wolfinger. Narrated by Stacy Keach. Boston: WGBH, 2002. Watch a team of firefighters as they battle to control one of the worst brush fires in the American West.

Unsolved History: Chicago Fire. DVD. Silver Spring, MD: Discovery Communications, 2003. This Discovery Channel documentary investigates the mystery of the Chicago Fire's beginnings. Did Mrs. O'Leary's cow really kick over a lantern, or has the cow been innocent all along?

Index

Photo Acknowledgments

The photos in this book are used with the permission of: NOAA News Photo/FEMA, p. 1; Bob McMillian/FEMA, p. 3; Bryan Smith/ZUMA Press, p. 4; © Royalty-Free/CORBIS, p. 5; Library of Congress, pp. 7, 28 (LC-USZC4-3788); © Ed Quinn/CORBIS, p. 9; © Laurence Fordyce; Eye Ubiquitous/CORBIS, p. 10; © SuperStock, Inc., p. 11; © Hulton Archive/Getty Images, pp. 12, 13 (both); © age fotostock/SuperStock, pp. 15, 39; Illustrated London News Picture Library, p. 16; Photo Disc Royalty-Free by Getty Images, p. 17; © Todd Strand/Independent Picture Service, pp. 18, 32 (both); © Katherine Bay/Jim Reed Photography/CORBIS, p. 19; Dave Saville/FEMA, p. 20; © David McNew/Getty Images, p. 21; Wisconsin Historical Society, WHi-1881, p. 22; © Bettmann/CORBIS, pp. 23, 29, 51, 57 (top); © Raymond Gehman/CORBIS, p. 24; © John Ruwitch/Reuters/CORBIS, p. 25; Andrea Booher/FEMA, pp. 30, 41; © Left Lane Productions/CORBIS, p. 31; © Bill Stormont/CORBIS, p. 33; Liz Roll/FEMA, p. 35; The Mariners' Museum, Newport News, VA, p. 36; Gustav Scholer Papers, Manuscripts and Archives Division, The New York Public Library, Astor, Lenox and Tilden Foundations, p. 37 (top); © Hulton Archives/Illustrated London News/Getty Images, p. 37 (bottom); © Underwood Photo Archives/SuperStock, p. 38; Karl Mondon/Contra Costa Times/ZUMA Press, p. 40; © FRANCISCO LEONG/AFP/Getty Images, p. 43; © DUNG VO TRUNG/CORBIS SYGMA, p. 45; AP/Wide World Photos, pp. 46, 47; © Bob Rowan; Progressive Image/CORBIS, p. 48; Cleveland State University Library Special Collections, p. 49; Ringo Chiu/ZUMA Press, p. 50; © Fred Greaves/Reuters/CORBIS, p. 53; © Lauren Wilken/Independent Picture Service, p. 54 (left); © Michael Klein/Visum/The Images Works, p. 54 (right); National Archives, pp. 55, 56 (bottom); © North Wind Picture Archives, p. 56 (top); © CHAIYANUWONG/AFP/Getty Images, p. 57 (bottom).

Front Cover: © Lucy Nicholson/Reuters/CORBIS; Back Cover: Liz Roll/FEMA.

About the Authors

Michael Woods is a science and medical journalist in Washington, D. C., who has won many national writing awards. He works in the Washington Bureau of the *Pittsburgh Post-Gazette* and the *Toledo Blade*. Mary B. Woods has been a librarian in the Fairfax County Public School System in Virginia and the Benjamin Franklin International School in Barcelona, Spain. Their past books include an eight-volume Ancient Technology series. The Woodses have four children. When not writing, reading, or enjoying their grandchildren, the Woodses travel to gather material for future books.